A Quiet Unwavering Soldier

VERNITA M. JACKSON

Copyright © 2025 Vernita M. Jackson. All rights reserved

Please note the information contained within this document is for awareness and educational purposes only. The events and conversations in this book have been set down to the best of the author's ability. No part of this book may be reproduced, stored in a retrieval system, or transmitted in any form or by any means, electronic, mechanical, photocopying, recording, or otherwise, without express written permission of the publisher.

ISBN: 979-8-9986757-2-0 (Paperback)

ISBN: 979-8-9986757-3-7 (Hardcover)

Published and designed by Ministry Event Marketing

Printed in the United States of America

Table of Contents

Introduction	7
Dedication	11
God's Plan	13
That's So Shay	15
Mother-Daughter Duo	17
Just For a Little While: A Mother's Remembrance	23
Unexpected Shift	31
The Missing Piece	35
The Dismissal	37
Vershayla's Message	39
Female Inspiration	41
Grief	43
Finale	45
A Note To A Queen	47
Dear God	49
Dear Daughter,	53
A Social Connection	57

Introduction

When an action occurs, we sometimes have the ability to make it happen. Not all actions are welcome with open arms. This book will show events that happened in the life of a young girl who was resilient throughout life all the way into her adult life. Even though she was sweet as chocolate cotton candy, her experiences weren't always pleasant. Her actions spoke for her; she was quiet in her demeanor but loud with her warm personality. She was always cheerful and had the most beautiful, enlightened, biggest smile.

As life happened, she faced multiple challenges that weren't always acceptable, and some were even painful, but she endured. She treated others like she wanted to be treated, even though she sometimes didn't receive as such.

Life wasn't always fair to her, but it had a purpose. She came across some obstacles that she had to face, some that she knew were beyond her control, but she also knew the power of prayer. She constantly prayed, fighting those things that were seen and unseen.

Her faith was unwavering, believing that a change was soon to come, so she kept pushing until something happened. Her mother was her best friend and biggest fan, who was always there through the ups and the downs. They were "two peas in a pod," and she would say, the best mother-daughter duo on this side of heaven. She loved her mother, and when you saw one, you saw the other not far away.

A shift began to occur that changed her world like never before. Her life turned in a direction with an unexpected invasion. It hit her like a ton of bricks, and she was facing her biggest fight ever.

Although it was not approved, she had no other choice. Her struggles were immensely real, but she knew how to overcome them by putting on the whole armor of God along with her pink boxing gloves. She was a quiet storm, always ready to win at every challenge. As she matured, life became more complex, but she remained in character no matter what she encountered. She had a mindset of not worrying because she knew "who she was and to whom she belonged" and where she was headed.

Dedication

This book is dedicated in honor of my daughter.

Vershayla Monique Munnerlyn,

who wanted her message to reach many and save lives. She definitely made an impact throughout her journey, and she will continue even from afar.

CHAPTER ONE

God's Plan

It was God's plan from the beginning of time to create each person in the image of himself with an intentional purpose. We each go through life with our own plans and agendas, sometimes with written programs, road maps, and our own perfect list of schedules.

Life can be filled with chaotic moments where we find ourselves encountering detours, stumbling blocks, and even interruptions that can throw us off course. Sometimes falling short on our journey may be because we feel it's too long, or perhaps the plan we have may not go as we expect, or perhaps because our agenda doesn't always fit the cause.

What matters the most as we travel on this journey is sometimes left out. We often fall short because God has not been acknowledged or is not given the authority to step in, but He is the most important, and doing things alone is harder than letting God lead. He will lead us in a direction already set for us.

Life requires the acknowledgment of God when we consent for Him to move in a direction that is best for us. He can make our lives smoother and less complicated, and we will win at every cost, no matter what. God's plan is the best, and it is not always pleasant; however, it's very vital with good reasons, and it matters. God's plan is not ours, so we have to move out of the way and let His will be done. He knows what's best, plus he created us only for His purpose.

CHAPTER TWO

That's So Shay

Vershayla was an angel sent from above. She was a daughter, sister, niece, cousin, goddaughter, and friend. She never met a stranger that she didn't have a heart for. To know her was to know that love really exists, as she exhibited it daily. She carried many other people's burdens as her own with a heart of gold.

She was pure to the core. She was a counselor to her peers and a prayer warrior. She was anointed a leader and a mediator, and she had a smile that was beyond beautiful and contagious to all around her. She was smart, independent, respectful, genuine, God-fearing, and full of life. She was a professional, a helper, and a light in dark situations.

She was a giver and gave without a thought and loved doing it.

Vershayla was a wise and obedient child. She had a cheerful spirit, always kind, very compassionate, respectful, trustworthy, and attractive in all aspects of her life— a diamond and a precious gem.

Vershayla was super sweet, her mom's favorite daughter, a masterpiece of beauty and love.

CHAPTER THREE

Mother-Daughter Duo

The day God gave me the gift of love, my life became your life, as I put my life on hold just for a little while.

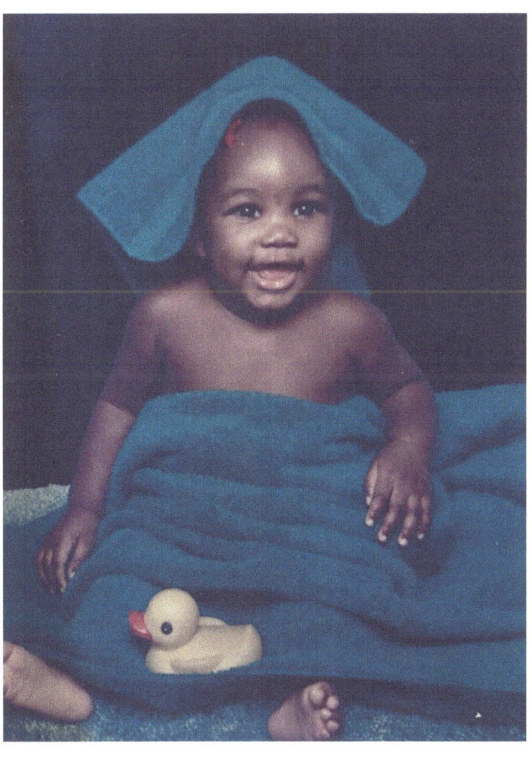

I didn't mind because it was a joy to see you enjoying and fulfilling life as you knew it. You kept me as busy as a bee, though, being active and involved in activities from those early morning soccer games, dance recitals, and first tee tournaments to all-day hot and steamy track meets.

That's what I called "EXTRA," and the list goes on.

I should have known you would be a busybody; even as a child you were a go-getter and always ready to go. Whenever anyone asked you, "Do you want to go?" your answer was always "Yes," or before they even asked, you would invite yourself.

As you matured, traveling became one of your favorite pastimes. We both often traveled together by car, plane, or on foot. We enjoyed each trip from New Orleans, the Bahamas, and Des Moines to Tennessee (Smoky Mountains) during those early times.

We embarked upon so many places, and if Covid

had not existed, we perhaps would have added Canada, but we will never know. Africa was on your bucket list, but I think by now you may have fulfilled that one. Everywhere we visited, you would say that would be the place you were going to move and set up residence, and to this day I'm not sure how serious you were.

You were such a comedian, always amusing others and making them laugh, but hey, what can I say? You got it, honestly. We were the best household team comedians; we came up with things that we knew people would say, "Hmm." We even put some of them on Facebook just to see people's responses. You were always ready to jump at those moments of silliness. What can I say about driving? You were happy when you learned to drive, and so was I. I remember you said how you were driving on the expressway, and apparently without my permission, I guess, I was taking it slowly, or baby steps, if you would, but I guess you knew what you could handle.

Not only were those good-ole' mom-and-daughter moments for the record, but those moments truly mattered and are forever embedded in my heart and soul.

I also reminisce about the two of us and the things we did, like going shopping. That was one of your favorite pastimes, always buying clothes, shoes, and jewelry.

We took strolls throughout the neighborhood, giving our surrounding neighbors' names because we didn't know them. Some other favorite pastimes were house painting and debating about Friday nights' dinners or just eating at a new or favorite restaurant.

When I became ill and spent time in the hospital, you didn't skip a beat. You were there from the start, and if you couldn't be there, you made sure someone was. After being discharged from the hospital, you researched this diagnosis of diabetes and the medications they had me on. You found herbs or something natural that would benefit me. Now I know for sure the true meaning of "ride or die." Being there with me, you wouldn't have it any other way. Just think, I had to sneak to shower, which sometimes worked because you insisted on making sure I was straight from washing my hair to my feet and checking those toe wounds. I would often say, "I got it," but you insisted and came anyway. You always made sure my health was on target.

I still have that image of you buying that homeless guy some water and a large pizza after seeing him with a bag of raw noodles and him placing water in the bag of noodles just to eat. Those are the kinds of things you don't see people doing because so many others are too busy and/or preoccupied with other things.

You even showed me how your actions exhibit what was in your heart, which is more than words can say. I was thinking after you said you were going to get some pizza for him that it would just be a slice, but I didn't feel as generous as you. You came back with a large pizza. I have seen you give your last. Those little, small actions of kindness go a long way, and they make a difference. We had an amazing, unique, and awesome bond, a win-win relationship like no other. It was special, and even now, through death, it can't be broken.

I was super blessed to have you in my life just for a little while, and I couldn't ask for a better daughter. We mattered together and had unforgettable memories. I truly miss you and our conversations, but God's plans are not ours. You saw my broken heart, and that morning when I stepped outside and looked down in the rocks, I saw an engraved heart. At that moment, I knew it was you watching over me. So, continue with those God winks and make my day. You will always be my forever 27 shining light.

CHAPTER FOUR

Just For a Little While: A Mother's Remembrance

I prayed for you, and God answered me. When I had my first ultrasound, there were two sacs, but only one developed. On that cool Monday afternoon, December 20th to be exact, you came as perfect as could be with beautiful skin tone, a full head of black hair, and sparkling oval eyes, turning those painful moments into a warm, contented substance of value. I realized at that moment that I had a responsibility for the next 18 years, but I was ready for the challenge. Not only did I pray for you, but God entrusted me with you, so I knew he equipped me for accountability. You made me a first-time proud mother, and my life forever changed. There was no turning back from that moment. You changed my life on that very day, but I had no idea that years later those changes would continue in such a way that would impact my life.

Gee, you taught me so much, including what love really means. Looking back to ages five, six, and perhaps seven, I often think about when you questioned me about things you didn't understand, like why people must pay for everything. You would obtain my answer but respond by saying, "When I grow up, I'm not going to charge people." You felt as though everything should be freely given, and little did I know, you were displaying the fruit of love at an early age. You had love for people, and for some reason you always gravitated to the ones that showed kindness, had good energy, and had a positive outlook on life. I guess you had a sense of discernment that was innately given just for you.

God used you at an early age, as I recall, in situations where you exhibited Christ-like character. You were always precocious for your age. I remember you creating songs, and you sang them around the house; however, I didn't take them seriously, nor did I have the desire to record them until years later when I thought about it.

From the start, your life was surrounded and full of love with family, church, pastors, and friends, just to name a few. I didn't think you knew anyone or anything could be different from what you were accustomed to. I thought about how it was almost time for you to step into the "world," or outside of the comfort of your home, knowing it was time for the big "K," kindergarten. You had been homeschooled with a curriculum not only with letters, math, colors, states, and capitals, but also the 23rd chapter of Psalm.

Starting school was just around the corner, and I was worried that once you started kindergarten, how would you handle others that may not be so lovable and kind, and I didn't want anyone to take advantage of you. So, I knew it was my job to enlighten you to stranger danger and to inform you that everyone is not kind or the way you were used to. I made sure you were prepared academically for kindergarten. Your kindergarten teacher often said how good your penmanship was.

She even let you nap past the regular time and often had you tying her shoes because you were good at it; I think you were her favorite.

You were always ambitious and a social butterfly. You connected with people so easily, and they enjoyed you as well as you enjoyed them. As each day evolved, I saw you growing, having fun, and enjoying life.

Dancing became your thing. On multiple occasions when the opportunity knocked and the doors opened, you would dance, and on other occasions, you recited the 23rd Psalm. You loved life, and life loved you.

When the new school year of 6th grade began as you were leaving elementary and going into middle school, you knew it was not only a new school but a new environment.

On the first day of class, I gave you the option of going in by yourself or me walking in with you. You chose and wanted me to walk in with you. You came home later that day, sharing how your first day of middle school wasn't so bad and how you met so many new people. You also shared how nervous you were and that you were glad I accompanied you.

Throughout those years you made many friends in middle school, plus you learned to play your first instrument, the clarinet. However, you loved your drama classes with those end-of-the-year big plays, staying after school for rehearsal and parties. You had so much fun, and you were so happy. Then it was soon time for another level and for you to step into high school. When you graduated from 8th grade, the tears kept falling, knowing the separation from your many friends was a heavy moment, but many said, "Don't cry, we will still be in touch." That was the love that you displayed all year long, and everyone around you saw and felt the same.

I can't forget how you loved singing, whether it was at school, in the church choir, or in a community choir. You sometimes teased and said, "I'm going on American Idol next year."

During your journey you met so many people that crossed your path, some for a season, some for a reason, and some for a lifetime. Your high school years were no different as you joined and participated in multiple activities, but band was your number one choice to top the list.

You played that clarinet throughout your four years of high school, and when your junior year came, you said you wanted to become the next year's drum major.

So, you set that goal, started working hard, and when it was time to audition for the drum major position, you were ready.

Not only did you make drum major, but you also became Lakewood's first Black female drum major. We were all proud of you. While being the leader of the band, you exhibited so many outstanding qualities, and those band members loved you, and that's because you stayed in that state of happiness, displaying acts of kindness, patience, and love.

You graduated from high school with the goal of attending college in Florida. Even though you had an opportunity to attend a college in Alabama, you decided to go elsewhere, stating that you didn't want to be far from your mom.

Months later we drove to Tallahassee, Florida, an experience in itself. You embarked on the college scene at FSU and later USF in Tampa, Florida. You got a chance to see how that world turned, and you accomplished much.

You were honored in the National Society of Collegiate Scholars and obtained your Bachelor of Arts degree in Communication Science and Disorders.

CHAPTER FIVE

Unexpected Shift

When cancer decided to knock on your door without consent, it was a bit shocking to us all. It was foreign to us as a family. We had never experienced this challenge; however, we learned later that you had the BRCA mutation from your dad's side. You knew it didn't come from your mother's side, but you wanted to make sure that your brother and I got tested, so you set an appointment with your doctor, and both results came back negative.

You were happy, as you were always looking out for us. Having cancer and going through that journey, I knew it was overwhelming, and perhaps fear may have set in, but as usual, you didn't want me to worry.

Through your struggle and pain, it was less about you, and I was your biggest concern. Many days when you weren't feeling well and when I left home, you would say to me, "Call me when you get there," just to make sure I reached my destination.

Nevertheless, even now I continue to feel your unconditional love surrounding me. You kept it real and positive, and now I look back and often say, "Thank you, God, for blessing me with a lovely daughter. I know you are not far away, looking down, giving a helping hand, and doing as much as you can, like you have done so many times before."

I think about how selfless you were even through your most difficult times. You were a strong warrior going through weeks of chemotherapy, expressing how you hated the taste it left in your mouth, feeling bad, losing your hair, still worried about others and how they were, and of course, checking on me. But God!

But through it all we learned to trust the process as God said, "Trust Me." After the first round of chemo, you smiled and said, "Now I can say I beat cancer."

Unfortunately, a couple of months later you experienced shortness of breath (SOB) and went to your doctor. After multiple tests and examinations, you learned that the cancer had spread to your lungs, pelvis, and abdomen. You said to me later that you didn't want to tell me and that you had sat in your car and cried for a while. You continued with more treatments, pills, and radiation, but nothing seemed to help or work, but as you said before, you knew "God was in the midst."

Even though things didn't go as I would have liked, God still answered our prayers, and he healed you completely. "TO GOD BE THE GLORY." He loved you so much, even more than I, and he called you home. (God's Plan). What a blessing to be in his presence in the fullness of joy and be free. I know that you had to go, and I have accepted the shift, but I'm still trying to digest and cope. When Vershayla said she completed phase one and moved into phase two, I don't think she knew it would be like nothing she had ever experienced. She said she would continue to fight and expect greater faith and be totally healed. She said she was crossing over to greater, walking into victory, and cheers to 2021.

God's Plan

CHAPTER SIX

The Missing Piece

God has rearranged some things, and now one piece of our puzzle is missing. It's a struggle, but I have accepted the shift and changes that have taken place, for it has left a void that is unable to be fulfilled. I know I can't bring you back, nor would you want to, but I can fight to get where you are.

I believe it is a place of awesome beauty, so these trials and temptations that I have to face keep reminding me that it is only a light thing, as it is written. So, until we reunite, the void remains, but we will meet again as I continue to fight with the whole armor.

You have set the stage and an example for me and others to see firsthand that the fight is worth it.

In your life, you showed us we can do all things with Christ, who strengthens us, and giving up is not an option.

Since you left your temporary home and moved into your permanent home, I feel like I'm just passing through. Everything looks and feels different, and nothing is familiar. I wake up every day now to a foreign feeling, but I push on to live. Your absence is bittersweet, but I know it's all good.

You have reached your final destination, obtaining your promotion with a fresh anointing. I know you are still smiling, with such joy, and living abundantly in a free world just like you wanted as a little child. I just know for sure you wouldn't change it. I remain faithful as I continue to walk "by faith, knowing that "God is in the midst" and this is His doing.

CHAPTER SEVEN

The Dismissal

Before Vershayla's diagnosis, she did everything right, from self-exams to speaking with her doctors about what she was experiencing and what she felt. She obtained ultrasounds and mammograms, but to no avail. They informed her that the cyst would dissipate or go away due to her young age.

They kept dismissing what she knew to be a problem. When she completed her first round of chemo, she expressed that she had beat the cancer and she was happy; however, it came back later and metastasized to her lungs, pelvic area, and abdomen.

CHAPTER EIGHT

Vershayla's Message

"Hi everyone, coming to you from the beautiful city of St. Petersburg, Florida. My name is Vershayla, and I'm 27 years old. I'm here to share my journey in hopes of helping others along the way. Last year I was diagnosed with stage three breast cancer.

After getting the news from my doctor, I felt like my life was coming to an end; everything around me just stopped. Being so young and receiving the devastating news, I didn't know what to do or what to expect. But I knew that God was in the midst somehow. My primary doctor lined me up with a host of doctors, and my journey began.

I went through chemo for four months, and just that experience alone was a lot to bear, but God! He got me through, and I'm so grateful to be here.

Now I look back, and I realize how blessed I am just to know that God was beside me every day, even when things got so rough or I thought I wasn't going to make it. But God! I am here to say, don't give up, hold on, and keep fighting for yourself because God expects you to fight too."

"I am Warrior."

CHAPTER NINE

Female Inspiration

Vershayla was always equipped for fighting fair no matter what came her way, and at an early age she decided to join God's Army. She knew from the start she was on the winning side, and she was content. She knew regardless of what she had to face, she would overcome it. She may not have known this final challenge would be as violent as it was, but she was certain that nothing was impossible with God. I always told her that God had us no matter what we encountered, whether good or bad. She listened attentively and gravitated to every word.

The last several years of her life included pain and suffering that affected her physically, emotionally, and perhaps mentally. The struggle was real, but she didn't give up or give in. She kept her faith, maintained a winning streak, and broke her own record.

Vershayla wanted to become an advocate for young girls, young ladies, and all women to reinforce the importance of knowing their bodies. She wanted everyone, especially females, to stay on top of their health. Don't take yourself for granted because she didn't want anyone to go through what she went through. She would want you to pay attention, and when your body speaks to you, please listen; don't let anyone tell you differently, follow what you feel, and demand what is needed.

She wouldn't want you to limit yourself but to save time and your life. Remember you are not too young, and good health matters. No sickness discriminates, nor does it have an age limit. So be inspired by her true-life events and be proactive, love yourself, and LIVE.

CHAPTER TEN

Grief

Vershayla lost the battle but won the fight. She fought hard, and even though our family and friends feel a void with broken hearts, we have wonderful memories. Oh, how I miss her like crazy, and as I think of her, I have to tell myself that she is happy, and once I say she is happy, then I smile.

This journey of grief that I have encountered is no joke; my strength comes from above and not from the world, and because I have strength, I understand.

For every parent who has lost a child, it's okay to be sad, but don't be angry. They are our loved ones, now, evermore, and forever in our hearts. God loved them even more, and their season of life ended in his plan.

God's plan is for everyone to live in the real world,

Heaven to be exact, that was created for us.

A world full of joy, peace, abundant love, beauty, and freedom, and where no pain or suffering exists. This paradise is what God has prepared for us—a place to look forward to when we, too, complete our journey. While we yet live and whatever burdens we have, God is near and He got us.

CHAPTER ELEVEN

Finale

After fighting the good fight of faith, on December 17, 2021, God decided to rescue Vershayla; therefore, he moved her residency to an upper level where she had no choice in the matter. Now she's free, happy, and living more abundantly with not a care in the world.

After tasting such, Vershayla wouldn't change it even if she could. She lives in heaven now, the place of love. If she had the opportunity to impart one piece of wisdom to the world, it would be to embrace the purpose of life, to follow the path that God has laid out for you, and to accept the things or actions that God sends, regardless of their pleasantness or unpleasantness, as he has a purpose for everything that transpires.

Don't take anything for granted; let God be the head of your life, get and stay in His will, complain not, and just trust His process.

Vershayla is right at home reaping all the love she once gave, a place of Love, Liberty, and Royalty. I can almost hear her say, "Mom, I want you to come; you would love it here."

CHAPTER TWELVE

A Note To A Queen

Vershayla passed away on December 17, 2021, and I received a text on December 19, 2021, just one day before her 28th birthday.

It goes as follows:

"Mom I could have never even hoped to express how much appreciation I hold in my heart for you, my loving mom.

You have helped me in the toughest of times, and you have celebrated by my side in the best of times. I am forever thankful for you and to you. Mom, in a million ways you showed me that you care.

I never doubt your unconditional love or that you will be right by my side, waiting patiently to catch me when I fall. How truly lucky I am to have a mom as giving and supportive as you are."

Your loving daughter,

Kershayla Munmorlyn

CHAPTER THIRTEEN

Dear God

I thank you for loving me beyond measure, that you died so I can live again once this temporary life is over. Many things happen that we just don't understand, and the process that you allow to manifest can sometimes be difficult and hurtful, but I trust you. As you know, I wasn't prepared when I lost my daughter, and it was really hard to bear. Each day was a challenge, and day upon day I didn't know if I could even face a tomorrow, not to mention the next minute or hour. As the sun rose and set, I forced myself to get up and move. I often felt like a zombie, just like the day when I lost my beloved.

Yes, I pray, and some days the pain is harder than others, but I continue to place this burden in your hands, so I put my trust in you. I can say this is the worst pain I have ever felt, and the nerves of Satan wanted me to get mad at you, but I refused because I knew better. I guess he didn't know who he was talking to because if I should get mad at anyone, it should be him, who comes to kill, steal, and destroy. I look to you, from whom my help comes, and I'm grateful to know that you will supply my every need and heal me accordingly. I know nothing happens without a reason, for I believe and trust every word that you have spoken, and I know you will keep me safe in your arms.

Dear God, please touch and heal everyone who is reading this book and perhaps who has lost a child or a loved one in general. Give them the strength and comfort that they need to carry on. Let wisdom have her perfect way in their lives with understanding and acceptance of the things they cannot change. Give them a special blessing and overflowing miracles. Embed in their hearts and minds the ultimate price you have paid in full for every pain, hurt, sickness, disease, salvation, and everything in between. Restore our broken hearts and increase our faith with the knowledge that you came to give us life and have it more abundantly.

Help us to accept our journey of your plans and focus on things above with your unconditional love that has no strings attached. Your joy, peace, and love have overtaken a place where we can live freely. Prepare our hearts and minds while we yet journey to contemplate on the plan you have for us, which is to prosper without harm, plus to give us hope and a Future (Jeremiah 29:11)

Amen

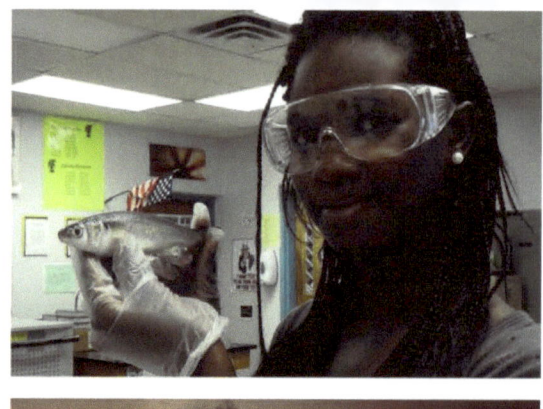

CHAPTER FOURTEEN

Dear Daughter,

Dear Shay,

As I look back and reminisce, I wouldn't change a thing. First, let me say that the world I have experienced is not what I expected. I find this world as fake as it comes, but to know that you are in the real world, a world that will never end, melts my heart. I can only imagine as you walk around Heaven and its fullness of blissfulness. Girl, you broke those chains, finished your course, and took off your gloves. It was a long, rough, and hard fight, but it was truly a knockout at the end, to say the least. Things still seem so surreal to me, and there has not been any interruption to the pain. You left a great legacy of lessons and many messages behind. It's some big shoes to fill, but I will follow you as I continue the journey on this side of Heaven. It's not always easy, but I look to the hills from which cometh my help, and I pull on God's strength. This has been one of the most difficult tests that I have ever encountered; perhaps I will have a testimony one day. However, I know you are right here with me as always. Remember you saw me in my mood of sadness, and you said in your soft, tender, weak voice, "Oh, Mom, I'm going to be alright," and you were right. I know you are because as you were transitioning, not only did our hands remain together, but you held onto God's hands, and to be absent from the body is to be present with the Lord. I see your smile. It is bigger than before, so that lets me know how joyful you are and living the life that you deserve and fought so hard for.

You are my shero, admired, firmly attached in my heart, my Black history that will never be erased.

Love,

Mom

My Mother's TIP:

LYMPH NODES are in the body to FIGHT INFECTIONS and should not be removed!!!

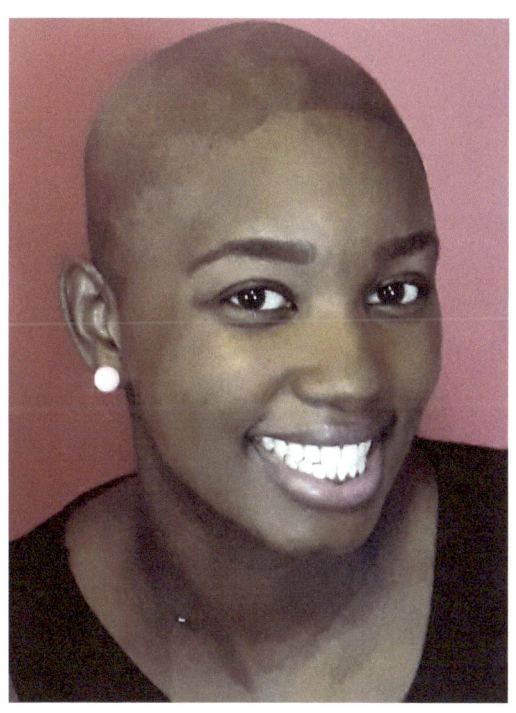

CHAPTER FIFTEEN

A Social Connection

As I scrolled through your Facebook page, I came across your post, and I read it with teary eyes. I will share it so others can read it too. Here is what it says:

> "Omg I can't believe that I made it to see not only the last day of the year, but I also completed my last chemo treatment. I am just filled with so many emotions right now!!!
>
> I want to give a SPECIAL SHOUTOUT to my AMAZING mother. When I tell you my mom has always gone above and beyond for her children, I mean just that!!! I truly appreciate you in every special way. We have laughed, cried, prayed, encouraged one another, always loved me unconditionally, genuine, caring and

so much more. Words cannot express how grateful I am for you and everything you do and continue doing. Your unconditional love, prayers, and outstanding support has always kept me going. Even when you weren't feeling your best some days, God gave me the strength to take care of you. I am extremely BLESSED to have you as my mother, and I love you to infinity and beyond always and forever,. Verni Jackson!!!

2020 has been a year...a year I will never forget. This journey has been extremely difficult, filled with many ups and downs. While going through chemo, I observed the trauma that my body went through along with the changes that occurred. This has truly been an experience and an eye-opener. My life was flipped upside down when I was diagnosed with stage three breast cancer that was extremely aggressive. It hit me like a ton of bricks!! Because the cancer was extremely aggressive, I had to receive the most aggressive treatment, and boy did my body suffer, and it even came close to me almost losing my life— but God.

I thank God for knowledge because if I hadn't stayed on the medical professionals and pushed testing and follow-up appointments, I truly believe I would not be here. I just want everyone to know that your health is important, and it matters! Please don't take things for granted, and if something in your body doesn't feel right, go and get checked out. Even if you and your doctor(s) are on two different pages about your health, no matter what, push the issue and stick to your gut feeling because no one knows and understands your body like you.

Due to my age I had to be my own advocate because no one believed cancer could affect a young woman in her mid-20s, not to mention *the symptoms that I was having were not problematic. If I knew then what I know now, I would have gone another route, but at that time I did everything in my power that I knew to do. Through it all I have grown through this process, and it has established me to another level.*

I know God has a purpose in my life, and even though finding out my diagnosis broke me, I can still say God entrusted me. This experience has made me so much stronger, and I know one day I will be able to help & encourage other young girls and women by telling them despite the situation or what it looks like, God is the only one who can turn the situation around. Not only that, know you can beat this and know you are stronger than cancer.

Praying for a better 2021 filled with good health, love, blessings, healing, abundance, and miracles. I still have a long road to recovery. But I'm not giving up, and I know God is truly right here beside me. I am just in awe of how good God is!! He has really kept me through all of this and has opened so many doors and continues to make a way. God is just so good!! Because of His grace, mercy, and love for me, I am still here. Phase one is finally over, and now I am moving on to phase two. Despite what it looks like, I know one day I will be totally healed. I am declaring it!! I am going to continue to fight and expect greater things. I know this too shall pass, and if God brought me to it, he sure can bring me through it.

I thank God for genuine family and friends who were there from the start. Because of you all, I don't know how I would have made it through. Thank you all for the outpouring of prayers, love, support, and concerns. It truly means a lot to me, and I am so grateful to have a huge, appreciative support system from so many loved ones. I just want you all to know that I am so grateful and appreciative for all of your generosity through this process. Cheers to Year 2021. Sending blessings to everyone!!!

#Testimony #CrossingOverToGreater #Tearscrieddidn'tmakemequit #BreastCancerWarrior #Godgiveshistoughestbattlestohisstrongestsodiers #WalkinginVictory!!"

Special Thanks

We thank everyone who was involved and supported us throughout this process/journey, whether near or far. We are forever grateful for your support, prayers, and, of course, love. Let us continue to spread Vershayla's message to others in hopes of making a difference in their lives.

MOM

"My whole life you have always been there for me. There will never be enough words to convey how deeply grateful I am that I have a mom as wonderful as you, but I can start with "I love you so much," influential woman in my life, my beloved Mom.

Whenever I am uncertain, I turn to you because you always guide me with your faith, hope, and love. Your support always helps to lift me up. Thank you for your never-ending patience and love, Mom.

Mom, throughout life, you have been my haven. Thanks to your valuable advice and stout character, I have had the best experiences in life."

With Love,

Kershayla Mummerlyn

www.ingramcontent.com/pod-product-compliance
Lightning Source LLC
Chambersburg PA
CBHW042341150426
43196CB00001B/17